D1572356

# WINTER NEWS

# WINTER
# NEWS

Poems by

JOHN HAINES

*Wesleyan University Press*

MIDDLETOWN, CONNECTICUT

"Prayer to the Snowy Owl," "The Dream of February," "The End of the Summer," and "Listening in October" were first published in *San Francisco Review Annual, I;* copyright © 1963 by New Directions; reprinted by permission from the publisher, New Directions.

I wish to thank the editors of *The Hudson Review,* for permission to reprint the following poems: "Stampede," "To Turn Back," "Poem of the Forgotten," "Winter News," "Poem for a Cold Journey," and "The Tundra" (originally entitled "The Battlefield"). I am grateful also to the editors of *Sparrow,* for permission to reprint "On the Divide," "Book of the Jungle," and "Denali Road"; to the editors of *Epoch,* for permission to reprint "Evening in Nenana" (originally entitled "Vesperae") and "Dream of the Lynx"; and to the editors of *The Massachusetts Review,* for permission to reprint "The Invasion," "The Traveler," and "The Cave of Animals."

Other poems in this book appeared originally in the following magazines: *Kayak, The Sixties, Oberlin Quarterly, Chicago Choice, Tampa Poetry Review, San Francisco Review, Wormwood Review, The Critic, Carolina Quarterly,* and *The Nation.* I am indebted to the editors of these magazines for permission to reprint.

Library of Congress Catalog Card Number : 66 – 14660
Manufactured in the United States of America
First Edition

FOR JO

# CONTENTS

I

# IF THE OWL CALLS AGAIN

at dusk
from the island in the river,
and it's not too cold,

I'll wait for the moon
to rise,
then take wing and glide
to meet him.

We will not speak,
but hooded against the frost
soar above
the alder flats, searching
with tawny eyes.

And then we'll sit
in the shadowy spruce and
pick the bones
of careless mice,

while the long moon drifts
toward Asia
and the river mutters
in its icy bed.

And when morning climbs
the limbs
we'll part without a sound,

fulfilled, floating
homeward as
the cold world awakens.

# WINTER NEWS

They say the wells
are freezing
at Northway where
the cold begins.

Oil tins bang
as evening comes on,
and clouds of
steaming breath drift
in the street.

Men go out to feed
the stiffening dogs,

the voice of the snowman
calls the white-
haired children home.

## POEM OF THE FORGOTTEN

I came to this place,
a young man green and lonely.

Well quit of the world,
I framed a house of moss and timber,
called it a home,
and sat in the warm evenings
singing to myself as a man sings
when he knows there is
no one to hear.

I made my bed under the shadow
of leaves, and awoke
in the first snow of autumn,
filled with silence.

# THE MOLE

Sometimes I envy those
who spring like great black-
and-gold butterflies
before the crowded feet
of summer—
                    brief, intense,
like pieces of the sun,
they are remembered and celebrated
long after night has fallen.

But I believe also in one
who in the dead of winter
tunnels through a damp,
clinging darkness,
nosing the soil of old gardens.

He lives unnoticed, but
deep within him there is a dream
of the surface one day
breaking and crumbling:

and a small, brown-furred
figure stands there,
blinking at the sky,
as the rising sun slowly dries
his strange, unruly wings.

Slowly, without sun, the day sinks
toward the close of December.
It is minus sixty degrees.

Over the sleeping houses a dense
fog rises—smoke from banked fires,
and the snowy breath of an abyss
through which the cold town
is perceptibly falling.

As if Death were a voice made visible,
with the power of illumination . . .

Now, in the white shadow
of those streets, ghostly newsboys
make their rounds, delivering
to the homes of those
who have died of the frost
word of the resurrection of Silence.

15

# THE HOUSE OF THE INJURED

I found a house in the forest,
small, windowless, and dark.

From the doorway came the close,
suffocating odor of blood
and fur mixed with dung.

I looked inside and saw an injured
bird that filled the room,
fluttering against the walls.

With a stifled croaking
it lunged toward the door
as if held back
by an invisible chain:

the beak was half eaten away,
and its heart beat wildly
under the rumpled feathers.

I sank to my knees—
a man shown the face of God.

# FOREBODING

Something immense and lonely
divides the earth at evening.

For nine years I have watched
from an inner doorway:
as in a confused vision,
manlike figures approach, cover
their faces, and pass on,
heavy with iron and distance.

There is no sound but the wind
crossing the road, filling
the ruts with a dust as fine as chalk.

Like the closing of an inner door,
the day begins its dark
journey, across nine bridges
wrecked one by one.

# TO TURN BACK

The grass people bow
their heads before the wind.

How would it be
to stand among them, bending
our heads like that . . . ?

Yes . . . and no . . . perhaps . . .
lifting our dusty faces
as if we were waiting for
the rain . . . ?

The grass people stand
all year, patient and obedient—

to be among them
is to have only simple
and friendly thoughts,

and not be afraid.

# THE INVASION

In the far north the sea
is beginning to freeze,
and groups of men are
gathering on the stony shore
in a white dust of snow.

Their bodies are heavy with furs.
They have strong brown faces,
and eyes used to
looking into great distances.

From small fires built among them,
thin smoke mingles
with the guttural language
they speak and blows
away toward the south . . .

The man is clothed
in birchbark,
small birds cling to his limbs
and one builds
a nest in his ear.

The clamor of bedlam
infests his hair, a wind
blowing in his head
shakes down
a thought that turns
to moss and lichen
at his feet.

His eyes are blind
with April,
his breath distilled
of butterflies
and bees, and in his beard
the maggot sings.

He comes again
with litter of chips
and empty cans,
his shoes full of mud and dung;

an army of shedding dogs
attends him,
the valley shudders where
he stands,
        redolent of roses,
exalted in
the streaming rain.

II

# A MOOSE CALLING

Who are you,
calling me in the dusk,

O dark shape
with heavy horns?

I am neither cow
nor bull—

I walk upright
and carry your death
in my hands.

It is my voice
answers you,

beckoning, deceitful,
ruse of the hunter—

at twilight,
in the yellow frost

I wait for you.

# HORNS

I went to the edge of the wood
in the color of evening,
and rubbed with a piece of horn
against a tree,
believing the great, dark moose
would come, his eyes
on fire with the moon.

I fell asleep in an old white tent.
The October moon rose,
and down a wide, frozen stream
the moose came roaring,
hoarse with rage and desire.

I awoke and stood in the cold
as he slowly circled the camp.
His horns exploded in the brush
with dry trees cracking
and falling; his nostrils flared
as, swollen-necked, smelling
of challenge, he stalked by me.

I called him back, and he came
and stood in the shadow
not far away, and gently rubbed
his horns against the icy willows.
I heard him breathing softly.
Then with a faint sigh of warning
soundlessly he walked away.

24

I stood there in the moonlight,
and the darkness and silence
surged back, flowing around me,
full of a wild enchantment,
as though a god had spoken.

# THE MOOSEHEAD

Stripped of its horns and skin,
the moosehead is sinking.

The eyes have fallen back
from their ports into the sleepy,
green marrow of Death.

Over the bridge of the nostrils,
the small pilots of the soil
climb and descend.

In the cabin of the skull,
where the brain once floated
like a ruddy captain,
there is just this black water
and a faint glowing of phosphorus.

# VICTIMS

The knife that makes long scars
in the flesh lays bare the bones—

pale trees in the forest of blood
where the birds of life and death
endlessly weave their
nests with straws of anguish.

There, the hunter and his quarry . . .

Parting the branches, the doomed
animal chokes on his own
breath, and sees, as in a red mist,
his own dripping carcass.

## DENALI ROAD

By the Denali road, facing
north, a battered chair
in which nothing but the wind
was sitting.
              And farther on
toward evening, an old man
with a vague smile,
his rifle rusting in his arms.

## THE FIELD OF THE CARIBOU

Moving in a restless exhaustion,
humps of earth that rise
covered with dead hair.

There is no sound from the wind
blowing the tattered velvet
of their antlers.

The grey shepherds of the tundra
pass like islands of smoke,
and I hear only a heavy thumping
as though far in the west
some tired bodies
were falling from a cliff.

29

## ON THE DIVIDE

I am haunted by
the deaths of animals.

Their frozen, moonlit eyes
stare into the hollow
of my skull; they listen
as though I had
something to tell them.

But a shadow rises
at the edge of my dream—

No one speaks;

and afterwhile the cold,
red mantle of dawn
sweeps over our bodies.

The animal, rising at dusk
from its bed in the trampled
grass—
         this is how it all began.

Far off the shaggy tribesmen
listened and fed their fires
with thorns.

Secret paths of the forest,
when did your children walk
unarmed, clothed only
with the shadows of leaves?

We are still kneeling
and listening; as from the edge
of a neglected field
there rises sometimes at evening
the snort of a rutting bull.

One half
lives in sunlight; he is
the hunter and calls
the beasts of the field
about him.
Bathed in sweat and tumult
he slakes and kills,
eats meat
and knows blood.

His other half
lies in shadow
and longs for stillness,
a corner of the evening
where birds
rest from flight:
cool grass grows at his feet,
dark mice feed
from his hands.

# THE CAVE OF ANIMALS

Some of them are so much alone:
the red cow with flowers
in her mouth, and the small,
shaggy horse who
has never known a rider.

But the furious bison are dancing,
the caribou are fording a river
whose banks shelter a sunrise.

The black bull of the night bellows,
and the white bull
of sunlight answers . . .

Dawn breaks over a yellow
silence in the earth.

# III

## DESERTED CABIN

Here in the yellowing
aspen grove
on Campbell's Hill
the wind is searching
a fallow garden.

I remember the old man
who lived here.
Five years have gone by,
and his house has grown
to resemble his life—
a shallow cave hung
with old hides, rusty
traps and chains,
smelling of eighty years
of unwashed bedding
and rotting harness.

I see him sitting there
now as he used to,
his starved animals gathered
about his bony knees.
He talks to himself
of poverty, cursing softly,
jabbing a stick
at the shadows.

The bitterness of a soul
that wanted only to walk
in the sun and pick
the ripening berries.

It is like coming home
late in the evening
with a candle in your hand,
and meeting someone
you had forgotten—
the voice is strange.

It is the cold autumn wind
stirring the frozen grass,
as if some life
had just passed there,
bound home
in the early darkness.

## PRAYER TO THE SNOWY OWL

Descend, silent spirit;

you whose golden eyes
pierce the grey
shroud of the world—

Marvelous ghost!

Drifter of the arctic night,
destroyer of those
who gnaw in the dark—

preserver of whiteness.

# DREAM OF THE LYNX

Beside a narrow trail in the blue
cold of evening the trap is sprung,
and a growling deep in the throat
tells of life risen
to the surface of darkness.

The moon in my dream takes the shape
of animals who walk by its light
and never sleep, whose yellow eyes
are certain of what they seek.

Sinking, floating beneath the eyelid,
the hairy shape of the slayer appears,
a shadow that crouches
hidden in a thicket of alders,
nostrils quivering;
and the ever-deepening track
of the unseen, feeding host.

# THE DREAM OF FEBRUARY

## I

In the moonlight,
in the heavy snow,
I was hunting along
the sunken road
and heard behind me
the quiet step
and smothered whimper
of something following . . .

Ah, tree of panic
I climbed
to escape the night,
as the furry body glided
beneath, lynx with
steady gaze, and began
the slow ascent.

## II

And dark blue foxes
climbed beside me with
famished eyes that
glowed in the shadows;

I stabbed with
a sharpened stick until
one lay across
the path with entrails
spilled, and
the others melted away.

41

The dead fox
moved again, his jaws
released the
sound of speech.

### III

Slowly I toiled
up the rotting stairs
to the cemetery
where my mother lay buried,

to find the open grave
with the coffin
tilted beside it,
and something spilled
from the bottom—

a whiteness that flowed
on the ground
and froze into mist that
enveloped the world.

## THE VISITOR

The door is open
and the shaggy frost-fog
bounds across the floor
and wraps itself about my feet.
Restless, it climbs
upon my knees; I feel
its breath deep in my bones.

A spirit in it wants
to draw me out past
the whitening hinges
into the cold, enormous rooms
where it lives.

Out there a flickering pathway
leads to a snowy grave
where something in me
has always wanted to lie.

Then let it take me,
a lost, shivering animal—
eyelids shut fast,
hands folded,
wrapped in a stillness made of
ice and starlit tears.

dark wings that brush
the foliage above us; the crunch
of hoofs in frost,
a river flowing
in the lonely voice of the coyote.

As they walk through the moonlight,

we come and go by the flare
of campfires, full
of ghosts with huge, wounded hearts.

# THE TRAVELER

### I

Among the quiet people of the frost,
I remember an Eskimo
from Holy Cross, walking one evening
on the road to Fairbanks.

### II

A lamp full of shadows burned
on the table before us;
the light came as though from far off
through the yellow skin of a tent.

### III

Thousands of years passed.
People were camped on the bank
of a river, drying fish
in the sun. Women bent over
stretched hides, scraping
in a kind of furry patience.

There were long hunts through
the wet autumn grass,
meat piled high in caches—
a red memory against whiteness.

### IV

We were away for a long time.
The footsteps of a man walking alone
on the frozen road from Asia
crunched in the darkness
and were gone.

45

## SNOWY NIGHT

This is like a place
we used to know,
but stranger
and filled with the cold
imagination of a frozen
sea, in which
the moon is anchored
like a ghost
in heavy chains.

# STAMPEDE

There are cold, bearded men
laboring through the winter night.
They climb the drifts
of a windy, starlit pass
with iron sleighs, and rough dogs
whining in harness.

Behind them, ships shrouded
in smoke and steam
unload by the light of bonfires.
Mingled with heavy thuds
and the creak of straining tackle,
ghostly voices float slowly upward,
whitening in the cold night air.

Beyond the pass small boats
lie on the shore of a lake,
half-filled with snow, their thin
sails stiff with ice.
The boatmen are fast asleep,
wrapped in furs and frozen sweat,
dreaming of gold
and the white land of promise.

## SOUTH WIND

I dreamed of horses in the night,
invaders with strong, sweating
bodies plunging through the cold.

The stars were suddenly hidden,
but dark manes flowed
with sparks, and on the black,
frozen hills the rushing air
soared like a forest on fire.

The thunder of their passage
broke down the walls of my dream.
I awoke in the ruined kingdom
of frost with a warm wind
blowing my hair, and heard about me
and in the distance
the heavy hoofs still pounding
as the wild, invisible army
overran the north.

# POEM FOR A COLD JOURNEY

On the road of the self-
contained traveler I stood
like one to whom the great
announcements are made.

In one hand I held
a hard, dry branch with
bitter, purple fruit;
in the other hand a small,
blue-and-yellow bird
whose closed eyes stared inward
upon a growing darkness.

Listening, I could hear
within myself the snow
that was coming, the sound
of a loud, cold trumpet.

## THE TREE

Tree of my life,
you have grown slowly
in the shadows of giants.

Through darkness and solitude
you stretch year by year
toward that strange, clear light
in which the sky is hidden.

In the quiet grain of your
thoughts the inner life
of the forest stirs
like a secret still to be named.

# THE COMING OF NIGHT

## I

The sea is lifting something
on the shores of darkness.

A slime of rumors and burial
that slides inland
and covers the sleeping waste.

## II

Ooze and watery silence.
Liquefying bones.

As it might be in a tomb
where the dead lie rotting
and listening—

a cold, sucking mouth
at the door of my dream.

IV

# POEM

The immense sadness
of approaching winter
hangs in the air
this cloudy September.

Today a muddy road
filled with leaves, tomorrow
the stiffening earth and
a footprint
glazed with ice.

The sun breaking through
still warm, but the road
deep in shadow;
your hand in mine is cold.

Our berries picked,
the mushrooms gathered,
each of us hides
in his heart a small piece
of this summer,
as mice store their roots
in a place
known only to them.

We believe in the life to come,
when the stark tree
stands in silence above
the blackened leaf;
but now at a bend in the road
to stop and listen:

strange song
of a southbound bird
overflows
in the quiet dusk
from the top
                of that tree.

# PICKERS

All day we were bent over,
lifting handfuls of wind and dust.

Scraps of some human conversation
blew by; a coffin on wheels
rolled slowly backward across
the field, and the skinned
bodies of the harvest were loaded.

A red cloud boiling up out
of the darkness became the evening.
Sentinels of a shattered army,
we drank bitter coffee, and spoke
of the field, the light, and the cold.

# THE END OF THE SUMMER

## I

Let the inhuman, drab machines
patrol the road that leads nowhere,
and the men with Bibles
and speeches come to the door,
asking directions—
we will turn them all away
and be alone.

We will not storm what barricades
they erect on the Cuban beaches,
or set forth on the muddy
imperial water—
at least we shall go to hell
with open faces.

## II

The sun keeps its promises,
sentry in the cloth of departure.
The forest is empty,
the people are gone, the smoky
paths are waiting the feet
of furred and silent soldiers.
Death, the surveyor,
plots his kingdom of snow.

## III

Subversive leaves, you fall
and litter the camps
of our enemies. Unheard-of wars
sweep down from distant
mountains, filling
the cemeteries of the unborn.

Survivors beat with pale hands
upon the windows;
their eyelids are closed
and their scars sealed
with gauze against the cold.

I stare across the threshold
of my home and feel the sudden
wind that rises
like the breath from a grave.

# SAYING GOODBYE ON THE YUKON

A dance of northern bees,
and flowers in a mist
like a gesture
of farewell—

You have the long
south road before you,
where trees
droop at noon and
snow never falls;

and I in an old garden
begin to shape
this lonely summer.

# POEM OF THE WINTRY FISHERMAN

At the foot of October
where the current narrows,
the salmon wait,
burning in the shallows—

blood-red, green and orange,
in the ice-blue glacier water.

Listen! you can hear
the long, slow pull of slush
against the banks,
deep rumble of stones.

I stand alone in the smoking
frost, a long hook poised,
and fling the bright fish up
the pebbled, icy bar
to quiver and lie still,
a sinking fire.

Sometimes the cold eggs spill
in the snow, glowing
like the eyes of foxes who wait
at sundown, when I shoulder
my catch and mount
the frozen twilight homeward.

Along the darkening river,
ravens grip their iron twigs,
shadows of
the hungry, shuddering night.

# THAW

This wind is like water
pouring through the passes,
bringing a smell of the south
and the drowned, weedy coast.
a place we've never seen.

Reports of gales and wrecked barges.
Three men lost for days
in an open boat;
the search suspended for
the lonely survivor
who crawls exhausted above
the clutch of the tide,
his hands outstretched to the moon
which sails slowly by.

This water floods over us
and surges far to the west,
to be lost in the frozen
plains of the hunters,
who awaken and listen in darkness,
guarding a smoky candle
against the silent
and relentless cold.

# WATCHING THE FIRE

Where are the Red Men?
They should be here. They saw the mound
of skulls glowing on the hearth.

For them the stone lamp flickered
and the drafty cave
was walled with visions.

The stories they told us were true,
we should have believed them:

a woman of brute form nurses her child—
wise eyes in a wrinkled skin,
forehead of horn—

he wears a necklace of fangs
and cries softly for flesh and blood.

## LISTENING IN OCTOBER

In the quiet house
a lamp is burning
where the book of autumn
lies open on a table.

There is tea with milk
in heavy mugs,
brown raisin cake, and thoughts
that stir the heart
with the promises of death.

We sit without words,
gazing past the limit
of fire into the towering
darkness. . . .

There are silences so deep
you can hear
the journeys of the soul,
enormous footsteps
downward in a freezing earth.

## ON THE ROAD

It is not good to be poor.
It is good to listen to the wind,

but not when you stand
alone on a road at night
with all your winter parcels,
like a mailbox waiting for
a postman who will never arrive.

The wind comes in carloads,
and goes by with a rushing
of lights and emptiness.

I think only of my home.
I have a pair of slippers for a wife
whose bare feet are waiting.

There is a light through the trees—
it is only a simple place,
with two souls strung together
by nerves and poverty.

It is not good to be poor—
and there are no coins in the wind.

# CHRISTMAS, 1962

A soft wind blows
across the islands of anger
and sadness.

The astonished refugee rises
and comes now,
bearing in his white hands
the strange, unshackled
gift of himself.

## THE GARDENER

His hoe makes a hush
as of a stone rolled away.

We who are standing here
in rows, green men,
small handfuls of death,

we hardly know this one
who tends us—
dark, inscrutable angel
whose step passes by.

## WHAT IS LIFE?

There are no roads
but the paths we make
through sleep and darkness.

An invisible friend: a ghost,
like a black wind
that buffets and steadies
the lost bystander
who thinks he sees.

# INTO THE GLACIER

With the green lamp of the spirit
of sleeping water
taking us by the hand . . .

Deeper and deeper,
a luminous blackness opening
like the wings of a raven—

as though a heavy wind
were rising through all the houses
we ever lived in—

the cold rushing in,
our blankets flying away
into the darkness,
and we, naked and alone,
awakening forever . . .

# EVENING IN NENANA

Now the people
of shadow awaken.

The brown bat
opens his eyes
and looks down.

In their small,
weathered houses
above the river

the Indian dead
yawn and stretch.

# THE TUNDRA

The tundra is a living
body, warm in the grassy
autumn sun; it gives off
the odor of crushed
blueberries and gunsmoke.

In the tangled lakes
of its eyes a mirror of ice
is forming, where
frozen gut-piles shine
with a dull, rosy light.

Coarse, laughing men
with their women;
one by one the tiny campfires
flaring under the wind.

Full of blood, with a sound
like clicking hoofs,
the heavy tundra slowly
rolls over and sinks
in the darkness.

# THE WESLEYAN POETRY PROGRAM

*Distinguished contemporary poetry in cloth and paper editions*

Alan Ansen: *Disorderly Houses* (1961)

John Ashbery: *The Tennis Court Oath* (1962)

Robert Bagg: *Madonna of the Cello* (1961)

Robert Bly: *Silence in the Snowy Fields* (1962)

Tram Combs: *st. thomas. poems.* (1965)

Donald Davie: *Events and Wisdoms* (1965)

Donald Davie: *New and Selected Poems* (1961)

James Dickey: *Buckdancer's Choice* (1965)

James Dickey: *Drowning With Others* (1962)

James Dickey: *Helmets* (1964)

David Ferry: *On the Way to the Island* (1960)

Robert Francis: *The Orb Weaver* (1960)

John Haines: *Winter News* (1966)

Richard Howard: *Quantities* (1962)

Barbara Howes: *Light and Dark* (1959)

David Ignatow: *Figures of the Human* (1964)

David Ignatow: *Say Pardon* (1961)

Donald Justice: *The Summer Anniversaries* (1960) (A Lamont Poetry Selection)

Chester Kallman: *Absent and Present* (1963)

Vassar Miller: *My Bones Being Wiser* (1963)

Vassar Miller: *Wage War on Silence* (1960)

W. R. Moses: *Identities* (1965)

Donald Petersen: *The Spectral Boy* (1964)

Hyam Plutzik: *Apples from Shinar* (1959)

Vern Rutsala: *The Window* (1964)

Jon Silkin: *Poems New and Selected* (1966)

Louis Simpson: *At the End of the Open Road* (1963) (Pulitzer Prize in Poetry, 1964)

Louis Simpson: *A Dream of Governors* (1959)

James Wright: *The Branch Will Not Break* (1963)

James Wright: *Saint Judas* (1959)